Count On It!

Five

WITHDRAWN

Dana Meachen Rau

Benchmark
New York

Five fingers.

Five toes.

Five shells.

Five rows.

Five dogs.

Five toys.

Five candles.

Five boys.

Five!

19

Words We Know

boys

candles

dogs

fingers

rows

shells

toes

toys

Index

Page numbers in **boldface** are illustrations.

About the Author

Dana Meachen Rau is the author of many other titles in the Bookworms series, as well as other nonfiction and early reader books. She lives in Burlington, Connecticut, with her husband and two children.

With thanks to the Reading Consultants:

Nanci Vargus, Ed.D., is an Assistant Professor of Elementary Education at the University of Indianapolis.

Beth Walker Gambro is an Adjunct Professor at the University of St. Francis in Joliet, Illinois.

Marshall Cavendish Benchmark
99 White Plains Road
Tarrytown, New York 10591-5502
www.marshallcavendish.us

Library of Congress Cataloging-in-Publication Data

Rau, Dana Meachen, 1971–
Five / by Dana Meachen Rau.
p. cm. — (Bookworms. Count on it!)
Summary: "Identifies objects that inherently come in fives and lists other examples"—Provided by publisher.
Includes index.
ISBN 978-0-7614-2970-8
1. Five (The number)—Juvenile literature. 2. Number concept—Juvenile literature. I. Title. II. Series.
QA141.3.R275 2009
513—dc22
2007024616

Editor: Christina Gardeski
Publisher: Michelle Bisson
Designer: Virginia Pope
Art Director: Anahid Hamparian

Photo Research by Anne Burns Images

The photographs in this book are used with permission and through the courtesy of:
SuperStock: pp.1, 17, 20TL Digital Vision; pp. 7, 21TR age fotostock; pp. 11, 20BL GoGo Images;
pp. 13, 21BR doll, top, duck Stockbyte; pp. 13, 21BR truck, boat Stockdisc. *Corbis*: pp. 3, 20BR Sean Justice;
pp. 5, 21BL Mika/zefa; pp. 9, 21TL Simon Jarratt; pp. 15, 20TR JLP/Jose L. Pelaez; p. 19 Jeremy Hardie/zefa.

Printed in Malaysia
1   3   5   6   4   2